J 796.8159
Wouk, Henry
Kung fu

Kid Pick!

Title: _____

Author: _____

Picked by: _____

_____

Why I love this book:

_____

_____

_____

_____

MARTIAL ARTS IN ACTION

KUNG FU

BY HENRY WOUK

Marshall Cavendish
Benchmark
New York

Other Marshall Cavendish Offices:
Marshall Cavendish International (Asia) Private Limited, 1 New Industrial Road, Singapore 536196 • Marshall
Cavendish International (Thailand) Co Ltd. 253 Asoke, 12th Flr, Sukhumvit 21 Road, Klongtoey Nua,
Wattana, Bangkok 10110, Thailand • Marshall Cavendish (Malaysia) Sdn Bhd, Times Subang, Lot 46, Subang
Hi-Tech Industrial Park, Batu Tiga, 40000 Shah Alam, Selangor Darul Ehsan, Malaysia

Marshall Cavendish is a trademark of Times Publishing Limited

All websites were available and accurate when this book was sent to press.

Library of Congress Cataloging-in-Publication Data

Colligan, Douglas.
Kung fu / Doug Colligan.
p. cm. — (Martial arts in action)
Includes index.
ISBN 978-0-7614-4937-9
1. Kung fu—Juvenile literature. I. Title.
GV1114.7.C66 2011
796.815'9—dc22
2010013842

Editor: Peter Mavrikis
Publisher: Michelle Bisson
Art Director: Anahid Hamparian
Series design by Kristen Branch
Illustrations by Janet Hamlin

Photo research by Candlepants Incorporated
Cover Photo: Shaolin Monastery, China. Eightfish/Alamy Images

The photographs in this book are used by permission and through the courtesy of:
Alamy Images: Imagemore Co., Ltd, 2; Losevsky Pavel, 6; Hemis, 10; Jon Arnold Images Ltd, 14; Pictorial
Press Ltd, 19; Laurie Strachan, 29; Imagemore Co., Ltd. , 30; Paul Ives, 33; Look Die Bildagentur der
Fotografen GmbH, 34; Imagemore Co., Ltd., 39; Robert Harding Picture Library Ltd, 41. *Corbis*: Bob Krist,
8. *The Bridgeman Art Library*: Arthur M. Sackler Gallery, Smithsonian Institution, USA /Transfer from the
National Museum of Natural History, Smithsonian Institution, 13. *Getty Images*: Cancan Chu, 15; Photo by
CBS Photo Archive, 17; Julian Finney, 20; John Eder, 22; Andy Crawford, 32; China Photos, 36; Siri Stafford,
42. *Janet Hamlin*: 25, 26, 27. *SuperStock*: Lonely Planet, 24; Robert Harding Picture Library, 37.

Printed in Malaysia (T)
1 3 5 6 4 2

CONTENTS

CHAPTER ONE

KUNG FU CLASS

DANA LIKED WATCHING martial arts movies with her brother, Tim. So when he decided to take classes in kung fu, she went to watch the class. It was not what she expected. Everyone was wearing what looked like comfortable pajama pants with wide legs, just like in the movies. But the class was quiet. There was no shouting or wild jumping around or people wildly kicking others.

The students began with a bow to the teacher. Then everyone stretched and did warm-up exercises that looked strange to Dana. The students and teacher rolled their heads around on their shoulders, swung their arms around in circles, and wiggled their hands. After that, the teacher led them in some simple movements.

KUNG FU IS AN ANCIENT MARTIAL ART THAT BOYS AND GIRLS OF
ALL AGES AND ALL ABILITIES CAN LEARN.

EVERY KUNG FU CLASS BEGINS WITH A FORMAL GREETING TO THE TEACHER.

The boys and girls in the class were concentrating hard. But they were having a good time. At the end of the class, everyone was smiling and looked relaxed. Dana decided to join the class.

During the next sessions, she was not sure she could keep up. There was so much to memorize. She felt a little clumsy trying to imitate the teacher. But after a few classes, and patient practice and repetition, she got better. Dana noticed some changes in herself. She was stronger and her **reflexes** were faster. She was a goalie for her soccer team, and she found that her improved reflexes helped her block more shots.

At first, her brother Tim had the opposite reaction. In the beginning, he was disappointed that there was no fancy fighting. He wanted to drop out of class, but his mother suggested he stay with it a little longer.

Tim did, and he saw changes in himself. Sometimes during practice he would be called on to demonstrate some moves to newer students. He liked doing that and realized he was not as nervous as he used to be when he had to stand up in front of a group. His **self-confidence** had improved.

Tim and Dana still think kung fu movies are fun to watch. They recognize some of the moves and can even do some of them themselves. But they also know that there is more to kung fu than impressive moves and are happy to be martial arts students.

THE HISTORY OF KUNG FU

KUNG FU HAS BEEN AROUND for a very long time. Experts do not know precisely when it started. Some think it may have been invented as far back as four thousand years ago. What is certain is that kung fu began in China and has been part of that country's culture for centuries.

THE AGE OF THE YELLOW EMPEROR

Around 2700 BCE the ruler of China, known as the Yellow Emperor, decided to train his troops how to fight enemy soldiers with their hands as well as with weapons. Eventually, they developed a special form of wrestling that used feet and hands to hit and block attackers. This fighting skill later became a sport called *Jiao Li,*

SOME BELIEVE THE IDEA OF FIGHTING USING HANDS AND FEET AS WEAPONS BEGAN AS A MILITARY SPORT.

which means strength and endurance. Many believe this was one of the inspirations for what today is called kung fu.

THE WARRIOR MONKS

The next important development in Chinese martial arts began in central China around 550 CE. It happened at a place called the **Shaolin Monastery**. The name Shaolin means "little forest" because the monastery was nestled in the woods at the foot of a mountain. The monks who lived there believed in **Zen Buddhism**. This is a religion that encourages its followers to live a simple life and be men and women of peace.

Even though they tried to seek peace, the monks learned how to defend themselves when they traveled. So around the middle of the sixth century, they devised a special way of fighting that used their hands and feet.

Over time, the temple became famous for its fighting techniques. Other monks came from all over to learn them. The techniques followed a philosophy called **Taoism**. People who follow Taoism believe that there is a balance in nature of hard forces, called yin, and soft forces, called yang. Water, for example, can be soft, or have yang, when it is a quiet pond. But it can also be hard, or have yin, when it is a raging river. Some forms of kung fu emphasized the "soft" part of fighting, like ducking or dodging an attacker. Other forms emphasized the "hard" parts, which include kicking and punching.

Kung fu spread throughout China after the sixth century. Different masters, called **sifus**, experimented with the moves and came up

Bodhidharma, The Mystery Monk

Early in the sixth century a Buddhist monk named **Bodhidharma** sailed from his country, India, to China and the surrounding areas to teach Zen Buddhism. His travels took him to the Shaolin Monastery. There he was shocked to see the monks were so weak they fell asleep during meditation. He went to a cave to think about what to do. Legends claim that nine years later Bodhidharma came out of the cave with eighteen special exercises for the monks to perform every day. Soon the monks became stronger, more energetic, and healthier. Those exercises, some say, became the basis of kung fu.

LEGEND SAYS BODHIDHARMA STARED AT A WALL IN A CAVE SO HARD HE BORED HOLES INTO THE STONE.

MONKS FROM THE SHAOLIN MONASTERY IN CHINA
CONTINUE TO CARRY ON THE TRADITIONS OF KUNG FU.

with their own variations. In the thirteenth century, warriors from Mongolia, which is a region north of China, defeated the Chinese and conquered their land. The Mongols declared it against the law for anyone to learn kung fu. This lasted until the fourteenth century when a group of Chinese overthrew the Mongols. These Chinese people established the Ming dynasty. During this time, kung fu returned and blossomed. The years that followed were the golden age of kung fu.

WARRIOR MONKS AT THE MONASTERY PUT ON SPECIAL SHOWS TO ENTERTAIN THE TOURISTS.

The Legend of the Eighteenth Chamber

A popular story about kung fu states that in order for a monk to be considered a kung fu master, he had to pass a special test. The test was to fight his way through eighteen chambers in a Shaolin temple. Each chamber tested a different fighting skill. When he got to the last one—the eighteenth chamber—the way out was blocked by a huge metal urn, or container, filled with hot coals.

The only way the monk could move it was to grab it in a bear hug and lift it out of the way. The urn had two metal handles. Each was carved with a dragon. When a monk picked up the red-hot urn, the handles burned his forearms. As a result, a dragon design was burned into the skin of his arms. Having those marks meant that the monk was a Shaolin master.

THE MANCHURIAN DARK AGES AND THE TWENTIETH CENTURY

Kung fu almost disappeared again in 1644. That was the year invaders from Manchuria, a large region between China and Russia, conquered China. The Manchurian rulers outlawed all martial arts training. The monks continued to train in secret.

The law lasted for nearly two hundred years until 1911, when the Manchurian government was overthrown. Once again, people were

ACTOR DAVID CARRADINE'S TV SERIES, KUNG FU, MADE THE MARTIAL ART POPULAR IN AMERICA.

allowed to practice traditional Chinese martial arts. Communists—people who believe in the political system of **Communism**—took over the Chinese government in the 1940s. Kung fu was banned again. Communists believed that kung fu belonged to the "old" China and did not fit with their plans for a "new" China.

KUNG FU GOES WEST

While kung fu was forbidden in China during the late twentieth century, it still became popular in other parts of the world. One reason was an American television show in the 1970s called *Kung Fu*. It was about the adventures of a Shaolin monk who wandered through the American Wild West. He had escaped to America to get away from assassins in China. The show was very popular and made people aware that there was such a thing as kung fu.

Around the same time, studios in Hong Kong began making kung fu action films. One of the most popular performers was a Chinese actor, Bruce Lee. He was a highly skilled martial artist who did his own stunts. After a few years, he became an international movie star.

KUNG FU TODAY

In the 1980s kung fu finally was allowed in China again. Today, the Shaolin Monastery is a popular tourist spot where the monks put on a display of martial arts for visitors.

In China today, many officials call kung fu **wushu**. It is actually a more accurate label because the word means martial arts. Even with its new name, wushu is not like the traditional kung fu, which

focused on fighting and self-defense. Today, people who participate in wushu competitions add acrobatic and dance moves, but there is no **sparring**, or fighting between opponents.

Unlike many other martial arts, kung fu is not an Olympic sport. The only martial arts allowed in the Olympic Games—so far—are the Japanese martial art of judo and the Korean martial art tae kwon do. Even so, kung fu—in all its forms—is practiced by many people in many nations. Many kung fu students participate in competitions to safely spar against other students. There are kung fu classes, clubs, and associations for people of all ages and all backgrounds. Techniques that began in one Buddhist monastery in China thousands of years ago are now part of a popular martial art around the world.

CHAPTER THREE

KUNG FU BASICS

KUNG FU CLASSES all begin with some sort of warm-up exercises. To make sure the students do not injure themselves, instructors will have the class do stretching exercises. These may include slowly rotating the head or swinging the arms around in circles to loosen the arms and shoulders. Everyone may also do some jumping jacks or stand on one foot then the other, to warm up leg muscles. Once the students are warmed up, the kung fu movements begin.

KUNG FU STANCES

All kung fu moves start out with a **stance**, or a specific way of positioning the body. This creates solid footing that makes it hard

EVERY KUNG FU POSITION REQUIRES TOTAL CONCENTRATION AND KNOWING HOW TO MOVE THE BODY QUICKLY AND PRECISELY.

EVERY CLASS SHOULD HAVE STUDENTS OF THE SAME AGE AND SIZE TO PREVENT UNNECESSARY INJURIES.

to be knocked off balance. It also positions people so they can defend themselves or attack efficiently.

The most common stance is the **horse stance**. The feet are apart, spread a little wider than the shoulders. Toes point straight ahead. A fighter squats down as though he or she is sitting on a horse.

The upper body is kept vertical, or upright. The eyes should look straight ahead. Both hands are closed up fists, with the knuckles up. The hands are held close to the waist and the elbows are back. Practicing this stance can help to build up leg muscles.

THE HORSE STANCE: ALL KUNG FU MOVES START
WITH THIS VERY POWERFUL AND STABLE POSITION.

Another common position is the **bow**, or forward, stance. The kung fu fighter takes a long step forward with either the right or left foot until the back leg is completely extended. The front toe points straight ahead and the back toe points to one side at a 45 degree angle. Both fists are at the waist. The upper body is upright and eyes are straight ahead.

THE BOW STANCE: THIS POSITIONS THE BODY TO DELIVER A BLOW TO A TARGET IN FRONT OF A PERSON.

In the **cat**, or empty, stance the fists are at the waist and the upper body is vertical. Eyes look straight ahead. The right or left leg is extended forward and only the big toe is touching the ground. Most of the weight is on the back leg. This position allows a person to swivel, or turn, quickly in many directions.

THE CAT STANCE: RESTING LIGHTLY ON THE TOES OF BOTH FEET LETS A PERSON PIVOT IN ANY DIRECTION.

Once a person is grounded in a kung fu stance, he or she can then properly perform different kung fu movements. Using their arms, hands, legs, and feet, kung fu students move forward, backward, or to the side to attack or defend themselves.

KUNG FU STYLES

Over the centuries, kung fu masters have continually tried to improve kung fu, attempting different types of moves. As a result there are many different kinds, or styles. They are generally divided into two main groupings. One is the **Northern style** and the other is the **Southern style**. These refer to the regions of China where they developed. Northern style fighters use a lot of kicks and a wide stance. Southern style fighters use their hands more and stand with their feet closer together.

Most types of kung fu practiced today are a blend of the Northern and Southern styles. Some forms of kung fu include special moves of their own. Many were copied from nature. The ancient masters knew that every creature, from large animals to bugs, has a natural enemy and each had to protect itself. By watching the animals in the wild, the masters were inspired to come up with different fighting tricks and new styles.

WING CHUN

The story behind the **Wing Chun** style of kung fu is about a Buddhist nun who watched a fight between a snake and a crane. Each animal cleverly dodged the other's attacks. The nun, who was already a skilled kung fu fighter, copied the snake and crane

A GOOD INSTRUCTOR WILL CONCENTRATE ON THE PROGRESS OF EACH STUDENT.

moves. Later, she taught these moves to another female kung fu expert named Yim Wing Chun. She became a famous teacher of those techniques, and the style has been known by her name ever since. It was the style favored by kung fu superstar Bruce Lee.

THE PRAYING MANTIS

In the seventeenth century, a monk named Wang Lang was frustrated because no matter how hard he trained he could not

THE EAGLE STANCE: MANY KUNG FU MOVES WERE DEVELOPED BY COPYING ANIMALS.

defeat his fellow monks. One day he was sitting in a garden when he noticed a praying mantis fighting a bigger insect. He took the praying mantis home and watched it. He studied how it defended itself when he poked at it with a chopstick. He saw that the secret to its defense was its quick steps and move of grabbing to get control of the attacker. Wang Lang incorporated these tricks into his kung fu. The next time he sparred with his fellow monks, he won.

THE WHITE CRANE

Legend says that four centuries ago, there was a female kung fu expert named Fang Chi-Niang. She was planting seeds in her garden when a white crane landed and started eating them. Furious with the bird, she tried to drive it off with a staff. But the bird cleverly protected itself with its long beak. Fang Chi-Niang forgot about being mad and instead studied its moves. Out of this meeting with the large bird came techniques that helped her defeat men twice her size. Today that style is identified as the **White Crane** style. It is known for its quick sidesteps and staying close to the opponent. Staying close makes it harder for the opponent to hit very hard.

MONKEY STYLE

In the early 1900s, a martial arts fighter named Kou Sze fought with a bad man in his village and accidentally killed him. Kou Sze was arrested and put in solitary confinement, which meant he was left alone and did not interact with other people. He spent his days looking out his cell window at a grove of trees where monkeys played and fought. Kou Sze incorporated the monkeys' moves into a method known as the Monkey style. A fighter using these techniques will drop to the ground, roll away from his enemy, and use a lot of kicks to knock his opponent off his feet.

THE KUNG FU APPROACH NEVER USES FISTS BUT RELIES ON POWERFUL STANCES AND SPEED.

The Ancient Salute

There are many styles and techniques but one thing that is the same for every kung fu student is the greeting, or the **salute**. A person makes a fist with the right hand, presses it into the open palm of the left hand in front of him, and bows. Traditionally, this is how a kung fu student greets his master or his partner in a sparring match. It is a gesture of respect.

How this salute came to be is a mystery. Some say it began as a substitute for the handshake. A kung fu warrior was always on the alert and this was safer than giving a possible enemy a hold of his hand. Others say it was a secret greeting used during the Manchurian rule of China. The people who used the salute were followers of the Ming dynasty—enemies of the Manchurians.

EVEN IN THE MOST DANGEROUS SITUATIONS KUNG FU FIGHTERS WOULD SALUTE EACH OTHER FIRST.

CHAPTER FOUR

KUNG FU AND YOU

ONE OF THE MOST IMPORTANT parts of learning kung fu is going to the right school. Many places advertise themselves as teaching all different kinds of martial arts, though some are better than others at teaching kung fu. Careful research is the key to finding a good school that suits you.

If you know someone who is taking kung fu lessons, ask what he thinks of the teachers, the classes, and the other students. Whenever you consider a school, before signing up, watch a few classes. Most places will allow this. Notice how many people each teacher has in a class. Ideally, there should be at least one instructor for every ten to fifteen students. If there are too many students for each instructor, you may not get enough personal attention.

Take note of the teachers of the different classes. Some schools

IN CHINA MANY CHILDREN LEARN THE ANCIENT ART OF KUNG FU FROM A VERY EARLY AGE. IT IS PART OF THEIR HISTORY.

THERE IS A MODERN VERSION OF KUNG FU, CALLED WUSHU. IT LOOKS MORE LIKE DANCE THAN A MARTIAL ART.

have older students, or even teenagers, lead beginner classes. These student teachers have usually practiced kung fu for many years, and older instructors are confident that they can show beginners the basics. Many young beginners are more comfortable with first learning from older students or people closer to their age. However, in some schools, this could mean that beginners might not get as high a level of instruction as long-term students who are taught by older teachers.

Whatever the age of the teachers, you should find out how much

STUDENTS AT THE FAMOUS WUSHU INSTITUTE NEAR THE SHAOLIN MONASTERY PERFORM MODERN KUNG FU.

experience the school has with students your age. Good teachers who work with young athletes know which workouts and exercises to avoid and which ones are safe. In kung fu, as in most sports, the wrong exercise, or one done for too long, can cause serious injury. A good teacher will always be respectful of a person's limitations and how much they can do without getting injured.

If you are just starting to learn kung fu, you should look for a class that is right for your age and level. The students in your class should be about the same size and age as you. There should not be a mix of adults or bigger kids and younger kids in the same group. People can get injured accidentally sparring with someone who is bigger or smaller.

If you are interested in a school, ask if you can take a few classes before you decide to sign up for a session of classes. Most places will let you do this at a discount, or even for free. You are going to be spending a lot of time with these teachers and pupils so you want to be in a place you like, and a place where you feel comfortable.

THE BENEFITS OF KUNG FU

Centuries ago people mainly used kung fu for self-defense. People still learn kung fu to defend themselves. However, many have discovered that kung fu can have other benefits.

HEALTHY EXERCISE

Experts and doctors all agree that part of being healthy means doing some form of exercise. Moving the body around in safe

A KUNG FU MASTER DEMONSTRATES THE GRACE AND BEAUTY OF THIS ANCIENT MARTIAL ART.

ways helps control weight, exercises muscles, and keeps the heart healthy. Even people with some physical disabilities can benefit from practicing certain types of kung fu. At a school called Natural Motion Martial Arts in Scarborough, Maine, teachers have developed a training program that teaches kung fu movements to people with disabilities. This helps them stay more fit and healthy. It gives them a sense of accomplishment and it is fun.

BODY STRENGTH AND SPEED

Many sports and exercises only work parts of the body. Safely practicing kung fu can benefit the whole body. Practicing stances like the horse stance, for example, builds strength for the legs. Exercises for the arms, like punching drills, develop stronger upper bodies. Many kung fu masters and experts say that, with careful practice, both leg and hand reflexes get faster. Not only does this make a person better at kung fu, but he or she can also improve in other sports, from volleyball to football.

SELF-ESTEEM AND SELF-CONFIDENCE

Some teachers feel that kung fu can have even better benefits than team sports. Sometimes, coaches and players are more worried about winning games than how each team member is doing. In kung fu, the focus is on each individual and how he or she progresses. Students make it to the next skill level because of what they did by themselves, not as part of a group. For that reason, each person can be proud when he or she improves his or her kung fu skills.

Being proud of accomplishments can help build self-

A SHAOLIN MONK AND STUDENTS: MEN LIKE HIM PRESERVED KUNG FU FOR THOUSANDS OF YEARS.

THE REAL VALUE OF KUNG FU, SAY PEOPLE WHO HAVE BEEN DOING IT FOR YEARS, IS THE PURE FUN OF IT.

confidence and good self-esteem. Students who feel good about themselves may be more willing to face challenges and learn from their experiences. One thirteen-year-old kung fu student said that before she started kung fu classes she was more likely to be a couch potato than to try new things. After taking kung fu classes for a few months, she said, "I became a lot more focused and confident."

DISCIPLINE

There are different styles of kung fu, and they all have dozens of moves. It takes hard work and concentration to learn them all. This means that each student has to have enough discipline to pay attention in class and to practice. Students also learn to respect their teachers and their fellow students. One kung fu instructor tells parents, "Martial arts will teach your children to persevere and you will probably soon see improvement in schoolwork and behavior as well."

Even though kung fu is centuries old, it still has a place in many people's lives today. Kung fu is very popular and will continue to be so in the future. At kung fu schools around the world, students get healthy exercise, develop confidence and good self-esteem, and make new friends, all while learning about this ancient martial art.

GLOSSARY

Bodhidharma—A monk who traveled from India to China and, according to legend, is responsible for bringing the basics of kung fu to the monks of the Shaolin Monastery.

bow stance—Also called the forward stance, this powerful stance gives the fighter a strong position from which to strike.

cat stance—Also called the empty stance, this position lets a person move quickly in many directions.

Communism—A type of political system in which the entire community or the government owns all property equally.

horse stance—The most fundamental stance in kung fu, in which the feet are wide apart and the body set low.

Northern style—A type of kung fu in which the fighter uses kicks to defend and attack while using a wide stance.

Praying Mantis—A type of kung fu inspired by watching a praying mantis fight in which a fighter uses quick steps and grabs his opponent to keep him off balance.

reflex—An automatic physical response to something, such as hand or foot striking out.

salute—A respectful way of greeting someone. In kung fu, the traditional salute is bowing to another with the right hand clenched in a fist inside the left hand.

self-confidence—Belief in oneself and one's abilities.

Shaolin Monastery—The ancient monastery in central China where early forms of kung fu were developed and perfected.

sifu—A kung fu teacher with a high level of skill.

Southern style—A type of kung fu fighting in which fighters mostly use their hands to defend and attack.

spar—To fight against an opponent.

stance—A specific way of positioning the body when standing up.

Taoism—A philosophy that teaches about a balance in nature of hard force, called yin, and soft force, called yang.

White Crane—A fighting technique in which the fighter stays close to an opponent so the opponent does not have room to punch.

Wing Chun—A style of kung fu based on the movements of a snake and crane. It is named after the female martial arts expert who made it popular.

wushu—The formal Chinese term for some types martial arts. Some wushu movements come from kung fu.

Zen Buddhism—A religion with believers who focus on meditation and prefer to live a simple life of peace.

FIND OUT MORE

BOOKS

Eng, Paul. *Kung Fu for Kids*. North Clarendon, VT: Tuttle Publishing, 2005.

Heinrichs, Ann. *Kung Fu and Tai Chi*. North Mankato, MN: Child's World, 2004.

O'Shei, Tim. *Kung Fu*. Mankato, MN: Capstone Press, 2008.

WEBSITES

International Kung Fu Federation
http://www.internationalkungfu.com

Shaolin Gung Fu Insitute
http://www.shaolin.com

Shaolin International Federation
http://www.shaolin.asia

INDEX

ABOUT THE AUTHOR

Henry Wouk lives in western Massachusetts. He has written more than a dozens books and writes for national magazines from Reader's Digest to National Geographic Traveler. He has been a practitioner of Tai Chi for more than ten years and has studied the martial art at the China Institute in New York City.